MILITARY MACHINES

HELICOPTERS

BY CHARLES MARLIN

WWW.APEXEDITIONS.COM

Copyright © 2025 by Apex Editions, Mendota Heights, MN 55120. All rights reserved. No part of this book may be reproduced or utilized in any form or by any means without written permission from the publisher.

Apex is distributed by North Star Editions:
sales@northstareditions.com | 888-417-0195

Produced for Apex by Red Line Editorial.

Photographs ©: Shutterstock Images, cover, 4–5, 9, 14–15, 16–17, 18, 29; DVIDS, 1, 21; US Army, 6; Militarist/Alamy, 7; Chief Petty Officer David Mosley/US Coast Guard/DVIDS, 8; US Navy, 10–11; Bettmann/Getty Images, 13; Mass Communication Specialist 2nd Class Askia Collins/US Navy/DVIDS, 19; Master Sgt. Becky Vanshur/US National Guard/DVIDS, 22–23; Staff Sgt. George B. Davis/US Army/DVIDS, 24–25; Airman 1st Class Sebastian Romawac/US Air Force/DVIDS, 26–27

Library of Congress Control Number: 2024941300

ISBN
979-8-89250-338-9 (hardcover)
979-8-89250-376-1 (paperback)
979-8-89250-448-5 (ebook pdf)
979-8-89250-414-0 (hosted ebook)

Printed in the United States of America
Mankato, MN
012025

NOTE TO PARENTS AND EDUCATORS

Apex books are designed to build literacy skills in striving readers. Exciting, high-interest content attracts and holds readers' attention. The text is carefully leveled to allow students to achieve success quickly. Additional features, such as bolded glossary words for difficult terms, help build comprehension.

TABLE OF CONTENTS

CHAPTER 1
TO THE RESCUE 4

CHAPTER 2
HELICOPTER HISTORY 10

CHAPTER 3
DIFFERENT JOBS 16

CHAPTER 4
FLYING A HELICOPTER 22

COMPREHENSION QUESTIONS • 28
GLOSSARY • 30
TO LEARN MORE • 31
ABOUT THE AUTHOR • 31
INDEX • 32

CHAPTER 1

TO THE RESCUE

Soldiers walk down a road. Suddenly, bullets rain down. The enemy is attacking. One soldier gets shot and injured. An officer radios a helicopter pilot.

Many helicopters can fly fast and far. They can quickly reach people who are hurt.

Some helicopters have only a few seats. So, soldiers sometimes ride on the outside.

The pilot flies toward the hurt soldier. She lands nearby. Her copilot gets out. He picks up the soldier and carries him into the helicopter.

STRONG SHIELDS

Helicopters have strong **armor**. It covers them on all sides. And their windows are made of tough glass. These parts can stop bullets and other attacks.

Helicopter armor can stop large 12.7-mm rounds.

The pilot takes off. She speeds to the nearest field hospital. Doctors there take care of the hurt soldier. Meanwhile, the pilot returns to the battlefield. She helps fight the enemy.

Some military helicopters only do rescues. The MH-65 Dolphin is one example.

Some military helicopters are mainly used for fighting. For example, the AH-64 Apache is an attack helicopter.

FAST FACT

AH-64 Apache helicopters can fire up to 650 rounds a minute.

CHAPTER 2

HELICOPTER HISTORY

Militaries first used helicopters in World War II (1939–1945). By the Korean War (1950–1953), helicopters became more common. They often moved soldiers and supplies.

During World War II, helicopters rescued soldiers and spied on enemies.

Militaries used thousands of helicopters in the Vietnam War (1954–1975). New kinds of helicopters had better engines. They had better **weapons**, too.

HUEYS

The US military used Huey helicopters during the Vietnam War. They carried troops and supplies. They also attacked enemies on the ground. More than 7,000 Hueys flew in Vietnam.

Militaries from 48 countries have used Huey helicopters.

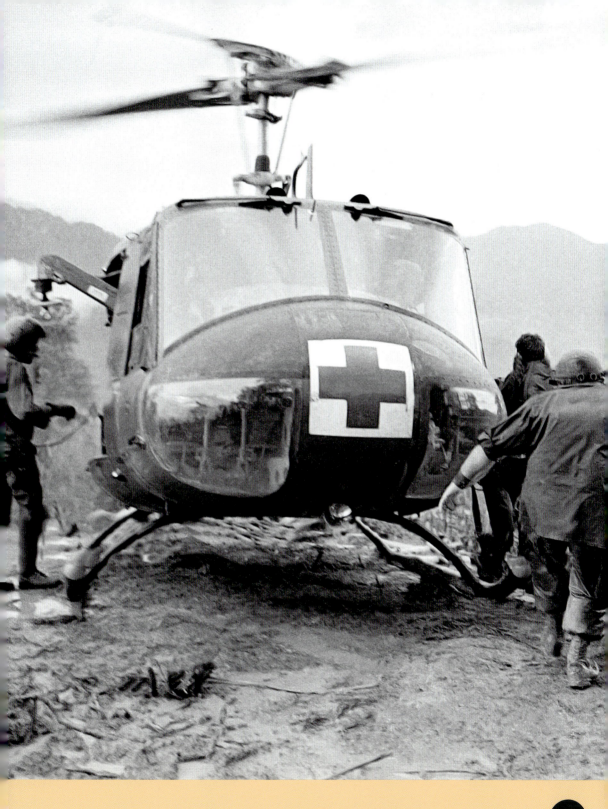

Over time, helicopters became faster and stronger. They could fly farther. Their **navigation** and weapon systems improved, too.

The UH-60 Black Hawk was designed in the 1970s. Militaries still use it today.

FAST FACT

Today, some helicopters can fly nearly 1,400 miles (2,300 km) without refueling.

CHAPTER 3

Different Jobs

Today, helicopters do many jobs. Transport helicopters move people and supplies. Rescue helicopters find lost or hurt soldiers.

The CH-47F Chinook is a fast transport helicopter. It can fly nearly 200 miles per hour (320 km/h).

Attack helicopters have powerful guns. Many carry **missiles**, too. They attack enemy soldiers and **vehicles**. The helicopters also **protect** ground troops.

AH-1Z Viper helicopters can carry 18 missiles.

Some helicopters drop torpedoes to hit underwater targets.

AT SEA

Some helicopters take off and land from ships. They help fight battles at sea. For example, they may drop torpedoes. These weapons can hit and sink ships.

Observation helicopters spy on enemies. They may fly over enemy land. They collect facts and pictures. Pilots send this information to soldiers on the ground.

FAST FACT

Some observation helicopters fly above battles. They track the enemy's location.

Many observation helicopters are small. Their size helps them hide from enemies.

CHAPTER 4

FLYING A HELICOPTER

Many helicopters have two-person crews. A pilot flies the helicopter. And a gunner controls the weapons. Sometimes, the gunner has a separate cockpit. It sits in front of the pilot's.

Helicopter cockpits have many screens and controls.

Helicopters use many types of sensors and cameras. They help people control weapons and steer. Many helmets have small screens. They show information from the sensors.

FAST FACT

Some helmets track the wearer's head movements. Cameras or guns point wherever the person looks.

Some helmet screens are small circles that go near one eye.

Helicopters can land and take off without runways. They can also fly far without refueling. So, they can often reach **remote** areas.

Helicopters can hover in one spot. Crews can bring people up into the helicopter without landing.

FLYING LOW

Helicopter pilots often fly low. That lets them sneak below **radar**. They also hide behind hills or buildings. That way, a radar's waves will hit these things instead of helicopters.

COMPREHENSION QUESTIONS

Write your answers on a separate piece of paper.

1. Write a few sentences describing the main ideas of Chapter 3.

2. Would you like to fly in a helicopter? Why or why not?

3. In which war were helicopters first used?
    - A. World War II
    - B. the Korean War
    - C. the Vietnam War

4. Why do helicopters have two-person crews?
    - A. The crew members can take turns flying.
    - B. Both people can fly and fire weapons.
    - C. Each person can focus on a separate job.

5. What does **tough** mean in this book?

*And their windows are made of **tough** glass. These parts can stop bullets and other attacks.*

    A. weak
    B. strong
    C. dirty

6. What does **sneak** mean in this book?

*Helicopter pilots often fly low. That lets them **sneak** below radar. They also hide behind hills or buildings.*

    A. move secretly
    B. move loudly
    C. crash

Answer key on page 32.

GLOSSARY

armor
Coverings that keep people or things safe.

missiles
Objects that are shot or launched as weapons.

navigation
The process of finding one's location and planning which way to go.

protect
To keep something or someone safe.

radar
A system that sends out radio waves to locate objects.

remote
Far away from towns or people.

vehicles
Things like ships, cars, and trains that people can ride in.

weapons
Things that are used to cause harm.

TO LEARN MORE

BOOKS

Gaertner, Meg. *US Air Force*. Mendota Heights, MN: Apex Editions, 2023.

London, Martha. *US Coast Guard Equipment and Vehicles*. Minneapolis: Abdo Publishing, 2022.

McKinney, Donna. *Apache Helicopter*. Minneapolis: Bellwether Media, 2024.

ONLINE RESOURCES

Visit **www.apexeditions.com** to find links and resources related to this title.

ABOUT THE AUTHOR

Charles Marlin is an author, editor, and avid cyclist. He lives in rural Iowa.

INDEX

A
Apache helicopters, 9
armor, 7
attack helicopters, 18

C
controlling, 22, 24

G
gunner, 22

H
Huey helicopters, 12

K
Korean War, 10

M
missiles, 18

O
observation helicopters, 20

P
pilots, 4, 6, 8, 20, 22, 27

R
radar, 27
rescue helicopters, 16

T
torpedoes, 19
transport helicopters, 16

V
Vietnam War, 12

W
World War II, 10

ANSWER KEY:
1. Answers will vary; 2. Answers will vary; 3. A; 4. C; 5. B; 6. A